Nurt _____ _____:

A Comprehensive Guide on Growing Nut Trees: Understanding the nuanced characteristics of each nut tree.

By

Daniel King

Disclaimer:

The material presented in this debate on "Nurturing Nut Trees: A Comprehensive Guide on Growing Nut Trees: Understanding the nuanced characteristics of each nut tree." is meant for general educational purposes only. It is not a replacement for expert agricultural advice on farming or regenerative processes. Always seek the assistance of a skilled professional with any questions you may have regarding any approach or technique provided in this guidebook.

Table of Contents

INTRODUCTION

Welcome to the fascinating world of nut cultivation! It is here that we witness the transformation of a humble seed into a mighty tree, bearing the promise of abundance and nourishment. In this guide, we embark on a journey deep into the heart of orchards, where we discover the art and science of growing nuts.

This journey goes beyond mere cultivation and embraces sustainability, community, and the joy of harvesting the fruits of your labor. The journey begins with a foundational exploration into the intricate world of nut trees. From the sturdy walnut to the delicate hazelnut, we explore the diverse varieties that grace our orchards.

Understand the nuanced characteristics of each nut tree, laying the groundwork for a successful and fulfilling cultivation experience. Beyond the allure of a bountiful harvest, growing nuts is a venture with profound benefits. Uncover the nutritional richness of nuts, delve into the economic considerations of nut cultivation, and explore the positive environmental impact that these trees bring to our ecosystems.

Not all nut trees are created equal, and selecting the right varieties is essential. Navigate the climate and soil requirements, consider regional factors, and acquaint yourself with popular nut varieties that suit your vision of a thriving orchard. Before the first seed is planted, meticulous planning is required. Dive into the considerations of selecting an ideal site for your orchard, preparing the soil, and understanding the role of sunlight and layout in fostering a healthy and productive nut haven.

A well-designed orchard is not just about rows of trees; it's a thoughtful ecosystem. Explore strategic layouts, companion planting techniques, and the importance of windbreaks in creating a nurturing environment for your nut trees. The birth of your orchard begins with the propagation of nut trees. Delve into the methods of seed propagation, master the art of grafting, and learn the intricacies of selecting and planting nursery trees to set the foundation for a thriving orchard.

As saplings find their home in the soil, understanding the best planting practices becomes paramount. Learn the nuances of planting and transplanting young nut trees, with a focus on fostering their early growth. Young trees require careful guidance to ensure a robust structure and future productivity. Explore the principles of pruning, provide support systems for growing trees, and train branches to foster the growth of healthy and resilient nut trees.

The foundation of a thriving orchard lies in the health of its soil. We'll explore the nutrient requirements of young trees, explore organic fertilization strategies, and discover the role of mulching in maintaining optimal soil conditions. As your nut trees mature, the art of pruning becomes both science and intuition. Explore structural pruning for tree health, discover techniques for enhancing yield, and tackle the challenges of disease and deadwood in a mature orchard.

Water is the lifeblood of your orchard, and efficient management is key. Dive into watering strategies, explore the benefits of drip irrigation systems, and learn to manage water effectively during dry spells to ensure the sustained health of your mature nut trees. No orchard is immune to pests and diseases, but strategic management is your shield. Familiarize yourself with common nut tree pests, master disease prevention and management, and implement integrated pest management techniques to foster a resilient orchard.

The culmination of your efforts lies in the joyous act of harvesting. Understand the signs of ripeness for different nuts, perfect your harvesting techniques, and grasp the timing for optimal flavor and nutritional content. The journey from tree to table involves careful post-harvest handling. Learn the art of drying and curing nuts, discover best practices for storage, and explore ways to process nuts for consumption, ensuring that the bounty of your orchard is savored to its fullest. Even the most seasoned orchardists face challenges. Explore common nut tree diseases and disorders, identify environmental stressors, and learn to recognize nutrient deficiencies to proactively navigate challenges in your orchard.

Resilience is the hallmark of a thriving orchard. Equip yourself with strategies to overcome challenges, embrace organic pest control methods, and adapt to changing conditions, ensuring the longevity and success of your nut-growing venture. As stewards of the land, sustainability becomes a guiding principle.

Dive into organic and eco-friendly practices, explore permaculture principles in nut orchards, and discover strategies for soil conservation that contribute to a sustainable and resilient ecosystem. Extend your orchard's influence beyond its borders. Engage with the community through educational initiatives, enhance biodiversity in your orchard, and explore ways to promote sustainable practices that reach beyond your individual trees. Nuts are not just a harvest; they are a culinary delight. Explore the diverse ways to cook with different nuts, create nut butters and oils, and discover how to incorporate nuts into everyday recipes, elevating your culinary experience.

Beyond the kitchen, nuts offer endless possibilities. Learn to make homemade nut milk, craft nut-infused beauty products, and utilize nuts in engaging DIY projects that extend the bounty of your orchard into various aspects of your life. Peer into the future of nut growing, where advancements in tree varieties, technology integration, and emerging trends promise a landscape of continuous innovation and growth.

As you tread this path of nut cultivation, become an ambassador for change. Engage in educational initiatives, collaborate on community projects, and promote sustainable practices to inspire a community of nut growers dedicated to cultivating a greener and more bountiful future. In concluding our journey through the vast orchards of nut cultivation, let these pages be your guide to the artistry and science of growing nuts. Whether you're a novice orchardist or a seasoned cultivator, the principles and practices unveiled in this comprehensive guide are crafted to enrich your experience and yield a bounty that extends beyond the confines of your orchard.

Nut Cultivation

Understanding Nut Trees

Nut trees, with their roots anchored deep in the soil, offer not only a harvest of delicious nuts but a glimpse into the intricate tapestry of nature's bounty. As we embark on this journey of nut cultivation, it is crucial to acquaint ourselves with the diverse varieties that make up the rich landscape of nut-bearing trees.

Walnuts (Juglans spp.):

The grandeur of walnut trees lies not only in their towering stature but in the nutritional richness of their nuts. English walnuts (Juglans regia) and black walnuts (Juglans nigra) are prominent varieties, each possessing a distinct flavor profile and culinary versatility. We explore the unique demands of walnut cultivation, from well-drained soil preferences to their preference for temperate climates.

Almonds (Prunus dulcis):

Almond trees, adorned with delicate blossoms, hold the promise of one of the world's most cherished nuts. Explore the cultivation nuances of sweet almonds and bitter almonds, understanding their distinct uses and the importance of pollination in the almond orchard.

Hazelnuts (Corylus spp.):

Hazelnut trees, with their whimsical catkins, contribute a delightful crunch to our culinary repertoire. Dive into the world of filberts and cobnuts, understanding their adaptability to various soils and climates. Uncover the secrets of hazelnut pollination and cultivation strategies that ensure a robust harvest.

Pecans (Carya illinoinensis):

The mighty pecan tree, native to North America, stands as a symbol of abundance. Delve into the peculiarities of pecan cultivation, from their preference for deep, well-drained soils to their sensitivity to chilling hours. Understand the art of managing water for pecan trees and unlocking the potential of this versatile nut.

Brazil Nuts (Bertholletia excelsa):

Originating from the Amazon rainforest, Brazil nut trees contribute not only to our culinary delights but also to the biodiversity of their native habitat. Explore the unique challenges and rewards of cultivating Brazil nuts, understanding their dependence on specific pollinators and the intricate dance between the tree and its environment.

Key Characteristics of Nut Trees

1. Growth Habit:

Nut trees exhibit a diverse range of growth habits, from the towering canopies of walnut and pecan trees to the more compact forms of hazelnuts and almonds. Understanding the growth habits of each variety is essential for effective orchard planning, spacing, and management.

2. Nutritional Content:

Beyond their delectable taste, nuts are nutritional powerhouses. Explore the unique nutritional content of each nut variety, from the heart-healthy fats of almonds to the omega-3 fatty acids abundant in walnuts. Appreciate the health benefits that make nuts an integral part of a balanced diet.

3. Pollination Requirements:

The intricate dance of pollination plays a pivotal role in the success of nut orchards. Some nut trees, like almonds, depend on managed pollination, while others, like hazelnuts, have distinct pollination strategies. Unravel the mysteries of pollination, from wind-pollinated hazelnuts to the fascinating interplay between bees and almond blossoms.

4. Soil and Climate Preferences:

Each nut tree variety has its own set of preferences when it comes to soil and climate. Walnuts thrive in well-drained soils with moderate moisture, while pecans favor deep soils and warm climates. Understanding these preferences is key to creating an environment where nut trees can reach their full potential.

5. Pruning and Training Needs:

Pruning is an art that shapes the structure and productivity of nut trees. Explore the pruning and training needs of different varieties, from the open-center pruning of almond trees to the careful management of the central leader in pecans. Mastering these techniques ensures not only a harmonious orchard but also optimal nut production.

Benefits of Growing Nuts

Nutritional Value

Cultivating nut trees is not just an agricultural endeavor; it's an investment in nutritional wealth.

Nuts are dense with essential nutrients, offering a symphony of vitamins, minerals, and healthy fats. Almonds, for instance, boast vitamin E and magnesium, promoting heart health and bone strength.

Walnuts, with their omega-3 fatty acids, contribute to brain function and cardiovascular well-being. Understanding the nutritional profiles of different nuts empowers growers to cultivate not only a bountiful harvest but a source of wholesome sustenance for consumers.

Heart-Healthy Fats:

Nuts are renowned for their heart-healthy fats, such as monounsaturated and polyunsaturated fats. These fats play a crucial role in reducing bad cholesterol levels, thereby lowering the risk of heart disease. The inclusion of nuts in a balanced diet becomes a proactive step toward cardiovascular well-being.

Protein Powerhouses:

For those seeking plant-based protein sources, nuts emerge as powerful contenders. Almonds, peanuts, and pistachios, among others, provide a substantial protein boost. This nutritional richness positions nuts as an essential component for individuals pursuing vegetarian or vegan lifestyles.

Economic Considerations

A Lucrative Harvest:

Beyond the nutritional benefits, the cultivation of nut trees holds economic promise. Nuts are high-value crops, commanding favorable prices in both local and global markets. The demand for diverse nuts continues to rise, presenting growers with the opportunity to not only meet consumer needs but also establish a lucrative agricultural enterprise.

Diversification of Income Streams:

Nut cultivation allows for the diversification of income streams within the agricultural sector. The ability to cultivate different nut varieties enables growers to tap into various markets, reducing the vulnerability associated with relying on a single crop. This diversification contributes to the resilience and sustainability of agricultural businesses.

Value-Added Products:

The economic potential extends beyond selling raw nuts. Entrepreneurs can explore value-added products such as nut butters, oils, and confections. Processing nuts into these products not only adds value to the harvest but also opens avenues for creative entrepreneurship within the nut industry.

Environmental Impact

Sustainable Agriculture:

Nut trees, with their perennial nature, contribute to sustainable agricultural practices. Unlike annual crops that require frequent replanting, nut trees offer long-term benefits. Their deep root systems contribute to soil health, prevent erosion, and enhance water retention, promoting overall sustainability in agriculture.

Carbon Sequestration:

The environmental impact of nut trees extends to their role as carbon sinks. As they grow, nut trees absorb carbon dioxide from the atmosphere, mitigating the effects of climate change. This dual benefit—nut production and carbon sequestration—positions nut orchards as allies in the global effort to combat environmental challenges.

Biodiversity Enhancement:

Nut orchards, when managed with biodiversity in mind, become ecosystems that support a variety of flora and fauna. Bees and other pollinators thrive in the presence of nut trees, contributing to the overall health of the orchard. Thoughtful orchard management practices further enhance biodiversity, creating a balanced and resilient agricultural landscape.

Choosing the Right Nut Varieties

Climate and Soil Requirements

Understanding the Nut's Home:

Selecting the right nut varieties for cultivation is akin to choosing the perfect abode for these perennial guests. Different nuts thrive in specific climate and soil conditions, making it crucial for growers to align their choices with the natural preferences of each variety.

Warm Embrace for Walnuts:

Walnut trees, such as the English walnut (Juglans regia), prefer temperate climates with distinct seasons. They thrive in areas with well-defined winters and warm summers, requiring a chilling period for optimal nut development. Well-drained soils that allow deep root penetration are ideal for walnut cultivation.

Almonds and Sunshine:

Almond trees (Prunus dulcis) are champions of warm climates with plenty of sunshine. They flourish in areas with mild, wet winters and hot, dry summers. Well-drained, sandy loam soils are well-suited for almonds, ensuring proper water drainage and preventing root diseases.

Hazelnuts' Versatile Spirit:

Hazelnuts (Corylus spp.) exhibit a versatile nature, adapting to a range of climates. They are particularly well-suited for temperate regions with moderate rainfall. While hazelnuts are resilient to cold temperatures, spring frost protection is essential for optimal nut development.

Pecans' Southern Charm:

Pecan trees (Carya illinoinensis) thrive in the warmth of southern climates, particularly in regions with hot summers and mild winters. Well-drained, deep soils are favorable for pecans, ensuring the roots have ample space to explore and access nutrients.

Amazonian Home for Brazil Nuts:

The Brazil nut tree (Bertholletia excelsa) is native to the Amazon rainforest, thriving in tropical climates with high humidity and consistent rainfall. These giants find their home in well-drained, nutrient-rich soils of rainforest ecosystems.

Considerations for Different Regions

Adapting to Local Nuances:

One of the keys to successful nut cultivation is understanding and adapting to the unique characteristics of the region. Considerations for different regions involve tailoring cultivation practices to the specific challenges and advantages presented by the local climate and geography.

Northern Challenges and Rewards:

In northern climates with colder winters, growers may face challenges such as late spring frosts, which can affect nut development. Selecting cold-hardy varieties and implementing frost protection measures become crucial strategies for success in these regions.

Navigating Arid Environments:

In arid regions, water management is a paramount consideration. Nut trees, especially almonds, must be strategically irrigated to ensure proper hydration without leading to waterlogged soils. Drip irrigation systems and efficient water management become essential tools for success.

Optimizing for Humidity:

In humid environments, such as the tropics, managing fungal diseases becomes a primary concern. Proper orchard spacing, adequate ventilation, and disease-resistant varieties play a pivotal role in overcoming challenges associated with high humidity.

Popular Nut Varieties

Almonds (Prunus dulcis):

Almonds are among the most popular and versatile nuts, cultivated extensively in regions with Mediterranean climates. California, with its warm, dry summers and mild, wet winters, stands out as a major producer of almonds globally.

Walnuts (Juglans regia):

English walnuts, with their rich flavor and culinary versatility, are cultivated in regions with temperate climates. Major walnut-producing regions include California, France, and parts of Eastern Europe.

Hazelnuts (Corylus spp.):

Hazelnuts find homes in a variety of climates, from the temperate regions of Oregon and Washington in the United States to parts of Europe. The Pacific Northwest, in particular, is renowned for its hazelnut orchards.

Pecans (Carya illinoinensis):

Pecans are synonymous with the southern United States, thriving in states like Georgia, Texas, and Louisiana. The warm climate and fertile soils of these regions contribute to the success of pecan cultivation.

Brazil Nuts (Bertholletia excelsa):

Native to the Amazon rainforest, Brazil nuts are predominantly cultivated in countries like Brazil, Bolivia, and Peru. The unique ecological requirements of the rainforest make these nuts a specialty crop in their native habitat.

Planning Your Nut Orchard

Site Selection and Preparation

Optimal Sunlight and Soil Conditions

1. Embracing the Sun:

Selecting the right site for your nut orchard begins with understanding the sun's role in nurturing your trees. Nut trees, being sun-loving entities, thrive in areas that receive ample sunlight. Optimal orchard locations have full sun exposure, ensuring that trees receive the sunlight required for photosynthesis, nutrient absorption, and overall healthy growth.

2. Nut Preferences for Soil:

The foundation of a successful nut orchard lies in the soil beneath. Different nut varieties exhibit specific soil preferences. While walnuts favor well-drained, loamy soils, almonds thrive in sandy loam. Hazelnuts appreciate moderately fertile soils with good drainage, and pecans find their home in deep, well-drained soils. Understanding these preferences is key to selecting a site that aligns with the nutritional needs of your chosen nut varieties.

Spacing and Layout

1. Orchestrating Harmony:

The layout of your nut orchard is akin to orchestrating a symphony, where each tree plays a vital role in the ensemble. The spacing and arrangement of trees impact sunlight penetration, airflow, and overall orchard management. Adequate spacing prevents overcrowding, facilitating better access to sunlight and reducing the risk of disease transmission.

2. Optimal Spacing Guidelines:

Consider the mature size of each nut tree when determining spacing. For instance, larger trees like pecans may require wider spacing to allow for their expansive canopy, while smaller trees like hazelnuts can be planted more closely. Guidelines for optimal spacing vary by nut variety and should be followed diligently to ensure healthy tree development and efficient orchard management.

Soil Testing and Amendments

1. Unveiling Soil Secrets:

Before planting the first nut tree, uncover the mysteries of your orchard's soil through comprehensive testing. Soil tests provide valuable insights into nutrient levels, pH, and composition, enabling informed decisions about amendments and fertilization strategies. Conducting soil tests is a proactive measure that lays the groundwork for a thriving orchard.

2. Addressing Nutrient Deficiencies:

Nut trees, like any crop, have specific nutrient requirements. Soil tests reveal potential deficiencies, allowing growers to tailor nutrient amendments accordingly. Whether it's adding organic matter to improve soil structure or supplementing specific nutrients, addressing deficiencies ensures that each tree receives the nourishment it needs to flourish.

3. pH Harmony:

Nut trees exhibit preferences for specific soil pH levels. While almonds thrive in slightly acidic to neutral soils, pecans prefer mildly acidic to neutral conditions. Soil tests guide pH adjustments, ensuring that the orchard's soil provides an environment conducive to nutrient uptake and optimal tree health.

4. Organic Matter and Soil Structure:

The presence of organic matter enhances soil structure, water retention, and nutrient availability. Amendments such as well-composted manure or cover crops contribute to the overall health of the orchard soil. Balancing organic matter levels ensures a fertile environment for nut trees to establish strong root systems.

Designing a Productive Nut Orchard

Orchard Layout Strategies

1. Embracing Efficiency:

The layout of your nut orchard is not just a matter of aesthetics but a strategic plan for maximizing efficiency and productivity. Orchard layout strategies involve careful consideration of tree spacing, row orientation, and overall organization. The goal is to optimize sunlight exposure, airflow, and ease of management.

2. Row Orientation:

Aligning rows based on the prevailing wind and sunlight patterns is a key consideration. East-to-west row orientation allows for uniform sunlight distribution throughout the day, ensuring that each tree receives its fair share of sunlight. This thoughtful arrangement minimizes shading and promotes even growth across the orchard.

3. Spacing for Access and Growth:

Balancing efficient access for orchard management with optimal spacing for tree growth is a delicate dance. Wider alleys between rows accommodate equipment and personnel, facilitating tasks such as pruning, harvesting, and pest management.

Simultaneously, providing adequate spacing between individual trees within rows ensures unhindered growth, ample sunlight exposure, and minimizes competition for nutrients.

Companion Planting in Nut Orchards

1. The Art of Companionship:

Companion planting in nut orchards involves strategically cultivating plants that complement the growth of nut trees. Thoughtful pairings can enhance nutrient cycling, attract beneficial insects, and deter pests. This symbiotic relationship contributes to the overall health and resilience of the orchard ecosystem.

2. Nitrogen-Fixing Companions:

Leguminous plants, such as clover or vetch, can serve as nitrogen-fixing companions in nut orchards. These plants have the ability to convert atmospheric nitrogen into a form that is accessible to nut trees, promoting healthy growth without the need for excessive synthetic fertilizers.

3. Pest-Repellent Companions:

Certain plants possess natural properties that repel pests harmful to nut trees. For example, planting aromatic herbs like rosemary or lavender can deter pests and create a more pest-resistant orchard environment. Companion planting with pest-repellent species reduces the reliance on chemical interventions.

Windbreaks and Shelterbelt Planning

1. Harnessing the Wind:

Windbreaks and shelterbelts play a crucial role in protecting nut orchards from the adverse effects of strong winds. Well-planned windbreaks can mitigate wind damage, reduce soil erosion, and create a microclimate that benefits nut trees. The orientation, height, and density of windbreaks should be carefully considered based on prevailing wind directions.

2. Native Trees for Wind Protection:

Incorporating native trees with dense foliage as windbreaks enhances their effectiveness. These trees serve as a natural barrier, reducing wind speed and turbulence within the orchard. Careful selection of windbreak species ensures compatibility with nut trees and the overall ecological balance.

3. Shelterbelt Planning for Microclimate Control:

Shelterbelts, consisting of a combination of trees and shrubs, are designed to create a sheltered microclimate within the orchard. They can modify temperature extremes, reduce frost risk, and shield nut trees from harsh weather conditions. Strategic planning of shelterbelts involves considering their placement relative to the orchard layout and the specific climatic challenges of the region.

Nut Tree Propagation

Methods

Seed Propagation

1. The Essence of Generations:

Seed propagation is the most fundamental method of bringing forth new nut trees. While it introduces a degree of genetic variability, it allows growers to preserve the unique traits of certain trees. Nuts collected from parent trees undergo stratification, mimicking natural winter conditions, before being planted in well-prepared nursery beds.

2. Selecting Superior Parent Trees:

To ensure desirable traits in the offspring, careful consideration is given to the selection of superior parent trees. Traits such as disease resistance, nut quality, and growth habits are evaluated. This method allows for the continuation of desirable characteristics from one generation to the next.

3. Challenges and Rewards:

Seed propagation introduces a degree of uncertainty due to the potential variability in offspring traits. However, it offers a cost-effective means of propagation and allows for the development of locally adapted varieties. It is particularly suitable for growers interested in exploring the potential diversity within a specific nut species.

Grafting Techniques

1. Preserving Desirable Traits:

Grafting is a technique employed to reproduce trees with specific, desirable traits by combining a scion (a shoot or bud) from a selected tree with a rootstock from another. This method allows growers to preserve the characteristics of superior nut varieties, ensuring uniformity in the orchard.

2. Techniques for Grafting:

Several grafting techniques are utilized in nut tree propagation. Cleft grafting, whip-and-tongue grafting, and bud grafting are common methods. Each technique has its advantages and is selected based on factors such as the type of nut tree, the size of the scion, and the desired outcome.

3. Ensuring Compatibility:

Grafting requires compatibility between the scion and rootstock. Nut trees within the same genus or species are generally compatible, but understanding the nuances of compatibility is crucial for successful grafting. This method allows growers to replicate superior varieties and accelerate the production of desirable nut trees.

Buying and Planting Nursery Trees

1. Expedited Orchard Establishment:

For those seeking a more immediate harvest, purchasing and planting nursery trees is a practical option. These trees are typically a few years old, having undergone initial stages of growth in a controlled nursery environment. Purchasing nursery trees expedites the establishment of an orchard compared to seed propagation or grafting.

2. Choosing Quality Nursery Stock:

Selecting high-quality nursery stock is pivotal for the success of the orchard. Look for trees with well-developed root systems, healthy foliage, and straight, sturdy trunks. Collaborating with reputable nurseries ensures that the trees are free from diseases and pests, setting the stage for a thriving orchard.

3. Planting Techniques for Success:

Proper planting techniques play a crucial role in the establishment of nursery trees. Digging adequately sized planting holes, ensuring proper depth, and backfilling with nutrient-rich soil contribute to the initial health and vigor of the trees. Attention to proper planting practices sets the foundation for robust growth in the seasons to come.

Nurturing Young Nut Trees

Best Planting Practices

1. Timing Is Everything:

Choosing the right time to plant nut trees is a critical first step. Ideally, planting is done during the dormant season, typically late fall to early spring, depending on the climate. Planting during dormancy allows the tree to focus on root establishment before the demands of the growing season.

2. Site Preparation:

Prepare the planting site meticulously to give young nut trees the best start. Clear the area of weeds, debris, and competing vegetation. Ensure proper soil drainage by amending heavy soils with organic matter. The depth and width of the planting hole should accommodate the tree's root system comfortably.

3. Correct Planting Depth:

Planting at the correct depth is essential for the tree's long-term health. The tree should be planted at the same depth it was in the nursery. Pay attention to the root collar, ensuring it sits just above the soil surface. Planting too deep or too shallow can impact the tree's stability and nutrient uptake.

4. Watering and Mulching:

After planting, provide a thorough watering to settle the soil around the roots. Apply a layer of mulch around the base of the tree, leaving a clear space around the trunk. Mulching helps conserve soil moisture, suppress weeds, and regulate soil temperature, creating an ideal environment for root development.

Transplanting Tips for Nut Trees

1. Choose the Right Time:

Transplanting nut trees requires careful consideration of the timing. Aim to transplant during the dormant season to minimize stress on the tree. This allows the tree to focus on acclimating to its new location without the additional demands of foliage growth.

2. Prune Wisely:

Pruning is a crucial step in the transplanting process. Remove any damaged or diseased branches, and consider shaping the tree to encourage balanced growth. Limit pruning to avoid excessive stress on the tree, allowing it to allocate energy to root establishment.

3. Minimize Root Disturbance:

During transplanting, minimize root disturbance as much as possible. Preserve the tree's root ball and handle it with care to prevent damage. A healthy root system is essential for the tree's ability to anchor itself in the new location and access nutrients and water.

4. Provide Adequate Watering:

Post-transplant watering is crucial for the tree's recovery. Ensure the soil around the transplanted tree remains consistently moist but not waterlogged. Adequate watering supports the establishment of new roots and helps the tree overcome transplant shock.

Caring for Bare-Root Trees

1. Timing and Handling:

Bare-root nut trees, with exposed roots, require special attention during planting. The timing of planting is critical, typically during the dormant season. Handle bare-root trees with care to prevent damage to the delicate roots. Prioritize planting as soon as possible after purchase to avoid drying out of the roots.

2. Soaking and Pruning:

Before planting, soak the bare-root tree in water for several hours to rehydrate the roots. Trim any damaged or excessively long roots. Pruning the tree's branches helps balance the ratio between the roots and the above-ground growth, promoting a healthy transition to the new location.

3. Planting Technique:

When planting bare-root trees, spread the roots evenly in the planting hole, ensuring they are well-distributed. Backfill with soil and water thoroughly to eliminate air pockets. Mulch the base of the tree to conserve moisture and suppress weeds.

4. Vigilant Monitoring:

Keep a close eye on bare-root trees during the initial weeks after planting. Regularly check soil moisture levels and water as needed. Monitor the tree for signs of stress or nutrient deficiencies, and take prompt action to address any issues.

Early Care and Training

Pruning Young Trees

1. Establishing a Strong Framework:

Pruning young nut trees is an art aimed at shaping a strong and well-balanced framework for future growth. Begin by removing any damaged, dead, or crossing branches. Encourage a central leader in the case of pecans and walnuts, or a well-defined scaffold structure for almonds and hazelnuts.

2. Timing of Pruning:

Pruning is most effective when conducted during the dormant season, typically late winter or early spring. This timing minimizes stress on the tree and allows it to allocate energy to healing and new growth. Avoid heavy pruning during periods of active growth to prevent excessive stress.

3. Training the Central Leader:

For species like pecans and walnuts, training a central leader is essential for creating a strong, upright trunk. Identify a dominant, well-placed shoot to become the central leader, and prune away competing leaders. Regularly assess the central leader's growth to ensure it remains the dominant vertical axis of the tree.

4. Encouraging Scaffold Branches:

Almonds and hazelnuts benefit from a scaffold structure comprising well-spaced, lateral branches. Encourage the development of these scaffold branches by selecting and training sturdy lateral shoots. Prune to maintain a balanced distribution of branches, preventing crowding and ensuring optimal sunlight exposure.

Support Systems for Growing Trees

1. Staking for Stability:

In regions prone to strong winds or in areas with sandy soils, young nut trees may benefit from temporary staking for stability.

Use sturdy stakes driven into the ground beside the tree and secure the tree to the stake with soft ties. Staking helps prevent wind-induced stress and allows the tree to establish a strong root system.

2. Tree Guards for Protection:

Protect young nut trees from potential damage caused by wildlife, mechanical injury, or herbivores by employing tree guards. These guards, typically made of plastic or mesh, create a physical barrier around the lower trunk, shielding it from harm. Regularly inspect and adjust tree guards as the tree grows.

Training Branch Structure

1. Guiding Limb Development:

Training the branch structure of young nut trees involves guiding the growth of limbs to create a balanced and open canopy. Identify well-spaced lateral branches and remove any competing or poorly positioned shoots. Encourage outward and upward growth to prevent a dense and crowded canopy.

2. Heading Back for Bushiness:

For certain nut trees, especially hazelnuts, heading back is a technique that promotes bushier growth. Heading back involves pruning the tips of branches, stimulating the development of lateral shoots. This method contributes to a more compact and productive tree shape.

3. Espalier Training for Space Efficiency:

In situations with limited space, consider espalier training for nut trees. This method involves training the tree to grow flat against a support structure, such as a trellis or wall. Espaliered trees are not only decorative but also make efficient use of space, making them suitable for small orchards or urban gardens.

4. Regular Monitoring and Adjustments:

Training branch structure is an ongoing process that requires regular monitoring and adjustments. Periodically assess the growth of branches, ensuring they follow the desired framework. Prune away any water sprouts or unwanted shoots to maintain an open and well-ventilated canopy.

Soil Health and Fertilization

Nutrient Requirements for Young Trees

1. Understanding Nutrient Needs:

Young nut trees, in their early stages of growth, have specific nutrient requirements crucial for establishing a strong foundation. The primary nutrients—nitrogen (N), phosphorus (P), and potassium (K)—play vital roles in various aspects of tree development. Nitrogen supports foliage growth, phosphorus aids in root development, and potassium contributes to overall vigor.

2. Micronutrients for Well-Rounded Health:

In addition to the primary nutrients, micronutrients such as iron, zinc, manganese, and copper are essential for addressing specific metabolic functions in young trees. Micronutrient deficiencies can manifest as chlorosis, stunted growth, or other symptoms, emphasizing the importance of a well-**balanced nutrient supply.**

3. Soil Testing for Precision:

Conducting regular soil tests is a proactive approach to understanding the nutrient profile of the orchard soil. Soil tests reveal nutrient levels, pH, and other critical factors. Armed with this information, growers can tailor fertilization strategies to address specific deficiencies and optimize soil health.

Organic Fertilization Strategies

1. Building Soil Structure with Organic Matter:

Incorporating organic matter into the soil is a cornerstone of organic fertilization. Well-rotted compost, cover crops, or organic mulches contribute organic matter, enhancing soil structure, water retention, and nutrient availability. Organic amendments support the development of a robust root system in young nut trees.

2. Cover Crops for Nutrient Cycling:

Utilizing cover crops, such as legumes, helps fix nitrogen in the soil through a symbiotic relationship with nitrogen-fixing bacteria. When the cover crops are incorporated into the soil, they release nitrogen, enriching the nutrient content and promoting a fertile environment for young nut trees.

3. Compost Teas for Microbial Activity:

Compost teas, brewed from well-made compost, are rich in beneficial microorganisms. Applying compost teas to the soil introduces a diverse community of bacteria, fungi, and other microbes. These microorganisms enhance nutrient cycling, improve soil structure, and contribute to overall soil health.

Mulching for Soil Health

1. Conserving Moisture:

Mulching is a valuable practice for conserving soil moisture, particularly during the dry seasons. Applying a layer of organic mulch around the base of young nut trees helps retain moisture in the root zone, reducing water stress and promoting optimal growth.

2. Suppressing Weeds:

Mulching acts as a natural weed suppressant, preventing the growth of competing vegetation around young nut trees. Weeds can compete for nutrients and water, hindering the establishment and growth of the trees. Mulch creates a weed-free zone, allowing young trees to access resources more efficiently.

3. Temperature Regulation:

Mulch serves as an insulating layer, regulating soil temperature by providing a buffer against extreme heat or cold. This temperature moderation is especially beneficial for the sensitive roots of young nut trees, fostering a stable and conducive environment for root development.

4. Organic Matter Contribution:

As organic mulch breaks down over time, it contributes to the organic matter content of the soil. This ongoing addition of organic material enhances soil fertility, microbial activity, and nutrient availability, fostering a thriving ecosystem around the roots of young nut trees.

Mature Nut Tree Care

Pruning Mature Nut Trees

1. Prioritizing Tree Structure:

Pruning mature nut trees is an essential practice for maintaining their structural integrity and overall health. Structural pruning involves shaping the canopy to encourage a well-balanced and open framework. Prioritize the removal of dead, damaged, or crossing branches to enhance air circulation and sunlight penetration.

2. Thinning for Light Distribution:

Thinning the canopy by selectively removing crowded or competing branches allows for improved light distribution within the tree. Adequate sunlight exposure is crucial for photosynthesis, fruit development, and overall tree vitality. Strategic thinning promotes uniform ripening and reduces the risk of disease in shaded areas.

3. Crown Cleaning for Airflow:

Crown cleaning involves the removal of deadwood, diseased, or insect-infested branches. This practice not only eliminates potential sources of infection but also enhances airflow through the canopy. Improved airflow reduces humidity within the tree, mitigating conditions conducive to fungal diseases.

Pruning for Improved Yield

1. Encouraging Fruiting Wood:

Pruning plays a pivotal role in stimulating the production of fruiting wood. Identify and retain well-positioned, vigorous branches capable of bearing fruit. Regularly remove excess, non-productive wood to direct the tree's energy towards the development of new, fruitful branches.

2. Renewal Pruning for Longevity:

Implement renewal pruning to invigorate aging nut trees and extend their productive lifespan. This involves selectively removing older, unproductive wood to encourage the growth of new, more vigorous shoots. Renewal pruning maintains the tree's capacity for fruit production and prevents a decline in yield over time.

3. Size Control for Orchard Management:

Controlling the size of mature nut trees is essential for efficient orchard management. Prune to maintain an optimal tree size, making harvesting, pest management, and overall care more manageable. Size control also prevents trees from shading each other excessively, ensuring that all parts of the canopy receive adequate sunlight.

Dealing with Disease and Deadwood

1. Prompt Removal of Diseased Wood:

Vigilant monitoring is crucial for identifying signs of disease in mature nut trees. Promptly remove any branches showing symptoms of disease to prevent the spread to healthy parts of the tree. Dispose of diseased wood properly to avoid further contamination within the orchard.

2. Deadwood Pruning for Safety:

Pruning out deadwood is not only vital for tree health but also essential for safety. Dead branches are prone to breakage and can pose a risk to both the tree and those working in the orchard. Regularly inspect mature nut trees for deadwood and eliminate potential hazards through targeted pruning.

3. Sterilizing Tools for Disease Prevention:

To prevent the spread of diseases between trees, sterilize pruning tools between each cut, especially when dealing with infected wood. A solution of 10% bleach or rubbing alcohol is effective for disinfecting tools. This practice minimizes the risk of introducing pathogens to healthy parts of the tree during the pruning process.

Irrigation and Water Management

Efficient Watering Strategies

1. Tailoring to Tree Needs:

Efficient watering strategies for mature nut trees involve tailoring irrigation practices to the specific needs of each tree. Consider factors such as soil type, weather conditions, and the tree's stage of growth. Different nut species may have varying water requirements, so it's essential to adapt watering plans accordingly.

2. Deep Watering for Root Development:

Encourage deep root development by implementing deep watering practices. Rather than frequent shallow watering, provide infrequent but deep watering sessions. This promotes the growth of a robust root system capable of accessing water stored deeper in the soil, enhancing the tree's resilience during periods of water scarcity.

3. Monitoring Soil Moisture:

Regularly monitor soil moisture levels to gauge the tree's water requirements accurately. Utilize soil moisture sensors or conduct manual assessments to determine when to irrigate. Adjust watering frequency based on seasonal variations, with increased watering during hot and dry periods and reduced frequency during cooler seasons.

Drip Irrigation Systems

1. Precise Water Delivery:

Drip irrigation systems offer a precise and efficient method of delivering water directly to the root zone of mature nut trees.

By minimizing water contact with foliage, drip systems reduce the risk of fungal diseases. The controlled release of water also prevents wastage and promotes optimal water use efficiency.

2. Installing Emitters Strategically:

Strategically install drip emitters to ensure uniform water distribution across the root zone. Consider the spacing of emitters based on the tree's canopy size and water requirements. Proper emitter placement guarantees that all parts of the root system receive adequate moisture, promoting balanced growth and productivity.

3. Utilizing Timers for Consistency:

Incorporate timers into drip irrigation systems to maintain consistency in watering schedules. Timers ensure that mature nut trees receive water at optimal times, reducing the risk of overwatering or underwatering. Consistent and well-timed irrigation supports the tree's health and minimizes stress, especially during critical growth stages.

Managing Water During Dry Spells

1. Implementing Water Stress Monitoring:

During dry spells, implement a proactive approach to water stress monitoring. Regularly assess the tree's physiological indicators, such as leaf color and turgor pressure. Early detection of water stress allows for timely adjustments to irrigation practices, preventing prolonged periods of drought stress.

2. Supplemental Watering in Drought:

In periods of prolonged drought, consider supplemental watering to alleviate water stress. Provide additional irrigation to compensate for reduced rainfall, focusing on maintaining soil moisture levels within the root zone. Adjust irrigation schedules based on the severity and duration of the drought to support tree health.

3. Mulching for Water Conservation:

Mulching is a valuable practice for conserving soil moisture during dry spells. Apply a layer of organic mulch around the base of mature nut trees to reduce evaporation, suppress weeds, and maintain a more stable soil moisture environment. Mulching complements irrigation efforts, promoting water conservation in the orchard.

Irrigation and water management are critical components of mature nut tree care, influencing overall health, productivity, and resilience to environmental stressors. By adopting efficient watering strategies, utilizing drip irrigation systems, and implementing thoughtful water management during dry spells, growers can contribute to the sustained well-being of their orchards.

Protecting Nut Trees from Pests and Diseases

Common Nut Tree Pests

1. Aphids:

Aphids are sap-sucking insects that can infest nut trees, causing stunted growth and transmitting diseases. Regularly inspect the undersides of leaves for clusters of aphids and monitor for the presence of honeydew, a sticky substance they excrete.

2. Codling Moths:

Codling moths are a common threat to nut trees, particularly walnuts. Larvae bore into nuts, causing damage and reducing yields. Pheromone traps and proper orchard sanitation are effective measures to monitor and control codling moth populations.

3. Walnut Husk Fly:

Walnut husk fly infestations can lead to the premature dropping of nuts. Monitoring traps and timely harvesting can help manage this pest. Proper disposal of fallen nuts can disrupt the fly's life cycle and reduce future infestations.

Disease Prevention and Management

1. Bacterial Blight:

Bacterial blight can affect nut trees, causing wilting, cankers, and dieback. Preventive measures include avoiding overhead irrigation, pruning infected branches, and applying copper-based sprays during the dormant season.

2. Walnut Blight:

Walnut blight is a bacterial disease that affects walnuts, causing dark lesions on leaves and husks. Regular copper-based fungicide applications during critical growth stages and pruning infected shoots help control walnut blight.

3. Phytophthora Root Rot:

Phytophthora root rot can be a concern in wet or poorly drained soils. Improving drainage, avoiding overwatering, and planting resistant rootstocks are preventive strategies. Fungicide treatments may be necessary in severe cases.

Integrated Pest Management Techniques

1. Beneficial Insects:

Encourage the presence of beneficial insects, such as ladybugs and predatory beetles, which naturally control pest populations. Planting flowering cover crops and minimizing the use of broad-spectrum pesticides help preserve these beneficial insects.

2. Trapping and Monitoring:

Utilize pheromone traps and sticky traps to monitor pest populations. Traps provide early detection, allowing for timely intervention. Regular monitoring helps identify pest trends and enables growers to implement targeted control measures.

3. Cultural Practices:

Implement cultural practices that reduce pest and disease pressure. Proper orchard sanitation, including the removal of fallen nuts and diseased plant material, disrupts the life cycles of pests and pathogens. Pruning to improve air circulation also minimizes conditions favorable for diseases.

4. Resistant Varieties:

Select nut tree varieties that exhibit resistance to common pests and diseases in your region. Planting resistant varieties is a proactive measure that reduces the reliance on chemical interventions and promotes sustainable orchard management.

Harvesting and Processing Nuts

Knowing When Nuts are Ready to Harvest

Signs of Ripeness for Different Nuts

1. Walnuts:

For walnuts, monitor the hull's color change from green to yellow. When the hulls start to split, revealing the nut inside, it's a sign of ripeness. Additionally, shaking the tree and observing mature nuts falling naturally is an indication that the majority of nuts are ready for harvest.

2. Almonds:

Almonds are ready to harvest when the hulls split open, exposing the inner shell. An additional indicator is the browning of the hulls. Shake a few branches, and if the majority of nuts fall, it's a signal that the almonds are ready for harvesting.

3. Hazelnuts:

Hazelnuts are mature when the husks change from green to a yellow-brown color. Additionally, the nuts will have filled out the husks, indicating plump and well-developed kernels. Harvest when the husks begin to crack open.

Harvesting Techniques

1. Hand Harvesting:

For smaller orchards or delicate nuts, hand harvesting is a common and precise method. Gently twist or snap nuts from the tree, being careful not to damage the branches or the nuts. Hand harvesting allows for selective picking of mature nuts.

2. Shaking and Collecting:

Larger orchards may use mechanical shakers to vibrate the tree, causing ripe nuts to fall to the ground. Collect the fallen nuts promptly to prevent damage or contamination. This method is efficient for nuts like walnuts and almonds.

3. Mechanical Sweepers:

In orchards with a significant nut crop, mechanical sweepers can be employed to collect fallen nuts efficiently. These sweepers gather nuts into rows for easy collection. This method is particularly effective for nuts like almonds.

Timing for Optimal Flavor and Nutrition

1. Balancing Ripeness and Flavor:

Timing is crucial for achieving the perfect balance of flavor and nutrition in harvested nuts. While nuts may be technically mature, allowing them to remain on the tree a bit longer can enhance flavor. Regular taste tests during the harvest season can help determine the ideal time for each variety.

2. Monitoring Moisture Content:

For certain nuts, such as walnuts, monitoring the moisture content is essential. Harvesting nuts when the moisture content is around 20% ensures that they are adequately hydrated for optimal taste and storage. Nuts with excessively low moisture content may lack flavor and become prone to storage issues.

3. Considering Nut Varieties:

Different nut varieties have unique flavor profiles and optimal harvesting times. Experimenting with harvesting times and noting the taste variations can provide valuable insights for future harvests. Keeping detailed records helps refine the timing for each specific nut variety in the orchard.

Processing Nuts

Cleaning and Sorting

1. Removing Debris:

After harvest, clean nuts by removing debris such as leaves, twigs, and hulls. This step is crucial for preventing contamination during subsequent processing stages.

2. Sorting by Size:

Sort nuts by size to ensure uniformity in appearance and roasting. This step is particularly relevant for nuts like almonds, where consistent sizing is desirable for both visual appeal and roasting efficiency.

Drying

1. Air Drying:

Allow nuts to air dry in a well-ventilated area. Spread them in a single layer on screens or trays to promote even drying. Air drying is a natural and energy-efficient method to reduce moisture content.

2. Commercial Dryers:

For large-scale operations, commercial dryers can be used to control temperature and humidity during the drying process. This ensures a consistent and efficient drying outcome, especially for nuts with specific moisture content requirements.

Storage

1. Cool and Dry Storage:

Store dried nuts in a cool, dry place to maintain their quality. Proper storage conditions help prevent mold growth, rancidity, and other issues associated with moisture. Ensure good air circulation to avoid any buildup of humidity.

2. Controlled Atmosphere Storage:

In advanced processing facilities, controlled atmosphere storage can be employed to optimize the storage conditions for nuts. This involves regulating temperature, humidity, and gas composition to extend the shelf life of nuts.

Shelling

1. Mechanical Shelling:

Large-scale nut processing often involves mechanical shelling equipment to efficiently remove shells. Mechanical shelling is precise and can handle high volumes, making it suitable for commercial nut processing.

2. Hand Cracking:

For artisanal or home processing, hand cracking may be employed. This method requires manual effort but allows for careful extraction of whole kernels.

Roasting

1. Enhancing Flavor:

Roasting nuts not only enhances flavor but also improves texture and aroma. Oven roasting or using specialized nut roasters can achieve the desired taste profile. Experiment with different roasting times and temperatures to find the optimal combination for each nut variety.

2. Seasoning Options:

Explore various seasoning options to add flavor to roasted nuts. Common choices include salt, spices, herbs, or sweeteners. Experimentation with seasoning profiles can create unique and enticing nut products.

Harvesting and processing nuts involve a delicate balance of timing, technique, and attention to detail. By understanding the signs of ripeness, employing appropriate harvesting techniques, and implementing careful processing steps, growers can produce high-quality nuts with enhanced flavor and nutrition.

Post-Harvest Handling

Drying and Curing Nuts

1. Air Drying:

After harvest, initiate the drying process to reduce moisture content and prevent mold or spoilage. Spread nuts in a single layer in a well-ventilated area. Air drying is a natural method that preserves the nuts' quality and flavor. Ensure even drying by turning nuts regularly.

2. Controlled Drying:

For precise control over drying conditions, consider using commercial dryers. These systems regulate temperature and humidity, providing an efficient and consistent drying process. Controlled drying is particularly beneficial for nuts with specific moisture content requirements.

3. Curing for Flavor Enhancement:

Curing involves allowing nuts to rest in a controlled environment after drying. This post-drying period enhances flavor and allows the nuts to develop their full taste potential. The duration of curing varies depending on the nut type, with some nuts benefiting from a few weeks of curing.

Storage Practices

1. Cool and Dry Storage:

Store dried nuts in a cool, dry place to maintain freshness and prevent spoilage. Adequate air circulation is crucial to prevent the buildup of humidity. Cool storage conditions help preserve the nuts' natural flavors and prevent rancidity.

2. Controlled Atmosphere Storage:

In advanced processing facilities, controlled atmosphere storage can be employed to optimize storage conditions. This involves regulating temperature, humidity, and gas composition to extend the shelf life of nuts. Controlled atmosphere storage is especially valuable for large-scale nut processing.

3. Packaging Considerations:

Choose appropriate packaging materials to protect nuts during storage. Use airtight containers or vacuum-sealed bags to prevent exposure to air, which can lead to rancidity. Transparent packaging allows consumers to inspect the nuts, while opaque or UV-resistant materials protect against light-induced quality degradation.

Processing Nuts for Consumption

Shelling

1. Mechanical Shelling:

For large-scale nut processing, mechanical shelling equipment is efficient and precise. This equipment removes shells rapidly and can handle high volumes. Mechanical shelling is commonly used in commercial operations for its speed and accuracy.

2. Hand Cracking:

Artisanal or home processing may involve hand cracking nuts. While more time-consuming, hand cracking allows for careful extraction of whole kernels. This method is suitable for smaller quantities and provides a hands-on approach to processing.

Roasting

1. Oven Roasting:

Oven roasting is a simple and accessible method for home processing. Spread nuts in a single layer on a baking sheet and roast in a preheated oven. Experiment with different temperatures and durations to achieve the desired flavor and texture.

2. Nut Roasters:

Commercial nut roasters offer precise control over the roasting process. These specialized machines ensure even roasting and can handle larger quantities.

Nut roasters are commonly used in commercial settings to produce consistently roasted nuts.

Flavoring and Seasoning

1. Natural Flavors:

Allow the natural flavors of nuts to shine by consuming them as-is. Many nuts have distinct and delicious flavors that can be appreciated without additional seasonings. This is an ideal option for those who prefer the pure, unaltered taste of nuts.

2. Seasoning Options:

Experiment with various seasoning options to create unique and flavorful nut products. Common choices include salt, spices, herbs, or sweeteners. Seasoning can enhance the taste profile and offer a diverse range of products for consumers.

Culinary Uses

1. Cooking and Baking:

Incorporate nuts into cooking and baking recipes to add texture, flavor, and nutritional value. Nuts can be featured in both sweet and savory dishes, from salads and granolas to cookies and casseroles.

2. Nut Butters and Spreads:

Process nuts into creamy nut butters or spreads. This versatile product can be used as a spread on toast, a dip for fruits and vegetables, or an ingredient in various recipes. Experiment with different nut combinations for unique flavor profiles.

Packaging for Distribution

1. Seal for Freshness:

Use packaging that ensures the freshness of processed nuts. Airtight seals, whether in bags or containers, prevent exposure to air and moisture, preserving the quality of the nuts over time.

2. Clear Labeling:

Clearly label packaged nuts with information on the nut type, processing method, and any added ingredients. Transparent packaging allows consumers to see the product, fostering trust and transparency.

Troubleshooting and Problem-Solving in Nut Cultivation

Common Challenges in Nut Cultivation

Nut Tree Diseases and Disorders

1. Bacterial Blight:

Bacterial blight affects several nut tree varieties, causing wilting, cankers, and dieback. Prevention involves avoiding overhead irrigation, pruning infected branches, and applying copper-based sprays during the dormant season.

2. Walnut Blight:

Walnut blight, caused by bacteria, manifests as dark lesions on leaves and husks. Control involves regular copper-based fungicide applications during critical growth stages and pruning infected shoots.

3. Phytophthora Root Rot:

Phytophthora root rot can be a concern in wet or poorly drained soils. Prevention includes improving drainage, avoiding overwatering, and planting resistant rootstocks. Fungicide treatments may be necessary in severe cases.

Environmental Stressors

1. Drought Stress:

Extended periods of drought can stress nut trees, leading to reduced growth and productivity. Implement supplemental watering during dry spells to maintain soil moisture levels within the root zone.

2. Excessive Heat:

High temperatures can cause heat stress in nut trees, affecting overall health and nut development. Provide shade, mulch around the base of trees, and ensure proper irrigation to mitigate the impact of excessive heat.

3. Frost Damage:

Late spring frosts pose a threat to nut trees, potentially damaging blossoms and young nuts. Implement frost protection measures, such as covering trees during frost events or using frost cloth, to minimize damage.

Identifying Nutrient Deficiencies

1. Nitrogen Deficiency:

Nitrogen deficiency manifests as yellowing of leaves, stunted growth, and reduced nut production. Address nitrogen deficiency by applying nitrogen-rich fertilizers or incorporating organic matter into the soil.

2. Phosphorus Deficiency:

Phosphorus deficiency can lead to delayed fruiting and poor root development. Apply phosphorus-containing fertilizers to address deficiencies, especially in soils with limited phosphorus availability.

3. Potassium Deficiency:

Potassium deficiency may cause leaf scorching, reduced nut quality, and susceptibility to diseases. Correct potassium deficiency by applying fertilizers containing potassium or incorporating potassium-rich organic amendments.

Problem-Solving Strategies

Integrated Pest Management (IPM)

1. Beneficial Insects:

Encourage the presence of beneficial insects, such as ladybugs and predatory beetles, to naturally control pest populations. Minimize the use of broad-spectrum pesticides to preserve these beneficial insects.

2. Trapping and Monitoring:

Utilize pheromone traps and sticky traps to monitor pest populations. Early detection allows for timely intervention, reducing the need for extensive pest control measures.

Soil Management

1. Soil Testing:

Regular soil testing provides insights into nutrient levels, pH, and other factors. Adjust fertilization strategies based on soil test results to address nutrient deficiencies and maintain optimal soil health.

2. Organic Matter Addition:

Incorporate organic matter into the soil to improve structure, water retention, and nutrient availability. Well-rotted compost, cover crops, and organic mulches contribute to the overall health of the soil.

Weather Adaptation

1. Weather Monitoring:

Stay informed about weather forecasts and trends. Regularly monitor weather conditions to anticipate potential environmental stressors and implement preventive measures as needed.

2. Microclimate Management:

Create microclimates within the orchard by strategically placing windbreaks, shade structures, or mulch. Microclimate management helps mitigate extreme temperatures and protects nut trees from adverse weather conditions.

Continuous Observation and Adaptation

1. Regular Orchard Inspections:

Conduct regular inspections of the orchard to identify signs of diseases, pests, or environmental stress. Early detection allows for prompt action and minimizes the impact on nut tree health.

2. Record Keeping:

Maintain detailed records of orchard management practices, weather conditions, and observed challenges. Historical records aid in identifying patterns and refining cultivation strategies over time.

Troubleshooting and problem-solving in nut cultivation require a holistic approach that addresses diseases, environmental stressors, and nutrient deficiencies. By implementing integrated pest management, practicing soil management, adapting to weather conditions, and maintaining vigilant observation, growers can overcome challenges and cultivate healthy, productive nut orchards.

Strategies for Overcoming Nut Growing Challenges

Resilience Building Practices

1. Diverse Cultivars:

Plant a variety of nut cultivars within the orchard to enhance resilience. Diverse cultivars may exhibit varying levels of resistance to diseases and pests, contributing to the overall health and stability of the orchard.

2. Rootstock Selection:

Choose rootstocks known for their resistance to specific soil-borne diseases. Resistant rootstocks provide a robust foundation for nut trees, reducing the risk of diseases such as Phytophthora root rot.

3. Crop Rotation:

Implement crop rotation practices to break disease and pest cycles. Avoid planting nut trees in the same location continuously. Alternating with non-host crops disrupts the reproduction and survival of specific pathogens.

Organic Pest Control Methods

1. Beneficial Insects and Birds:

Encourage the presence of beneficial insects, such as ladybugs, lacewings, and predatory beetles, which naturally prey on pests. Birds like bluebirds and titmice also contribute to pest control by consuming insects.

2. Neem Oil and Insecticidal Soaps:

Use organic insecticides like neem oil and insecticidal soaps to control common pests. These products are effective against aphids, mites, and certain caterpillars while minimizing harm to beneficial insects.

3. Companion Planting:

Strategically plant companion crops that deter pests or attract beneficial insects. For example, planting aromatic herbs like basil and mint may help repel pests, while flowering plants can attract pollinators and natural predators.

Adapting to Changing Conditions

1. Climate-Resilient Varieties:

Select nut tree varieties bred for climate resilience. Climate-resilient varieties are adapted to withstand changing weather patterns, including temperature fluctuations and unpredictable precipitation.

2. Water Management Strategies:

Implement efficient water management practices to address changing precipitation patterns. This may include adjusting irrigation schedules, optimizing water use, and exploring drought-resistant varieties.

3. Microclimate Modification:

Modify the microclimate within the orchard to provide protection against extreme conditions. Consider using shade structures, windbreaks, or mulching to create microclimates that buffer against temperature extremes and reduce stress on nut trees.

Continuous Learning and Adaptation

1. Stay Informed:

Stay abreast of the latest research, industry developments, and local climate trends. Regularly update your knowledge on nut cultivation practices to incorporate new and effective strategies.

2. Networking and Collaboration:

Connect with other nut growers, agricultural extension services, and research institutions. Networking provides opportunities to share experiences, learn from others, and access valuable resources for overcoming challenges.

3. Adaptive Management:

Embrace adaptive management principles by continually assessing and adjusting orchard practices based on observed outcomes. Flexibility and a willingness to modify strategies in response to changing conditions are key to sustained success.

Troubleshooting challenges in nut cultivation requires a proactive and adaptable approach. By incorporating resilience-building practices, utilizing organic pest control methods, and adapting cultivation strategies to changing conditions, nut growers can navigate uncertainties and foster the long-term health of their orchards.

Growing Nuts Sustainably

Sustainable Nut Orchard Management

Organic and Eco-Friendly Practices

1. Soil Health Enhancement:

Prioritize soil health through the incorporation of organic matter, cover cropping, and reduced tillage. Healthy soils foster nutrient availability, water retention, and microbial activity.

2. Natural Pest Control:

Encourage the presence of natural predators and beneficial insects to control pest populations. Employ companion planting strategies and utilize organic pest control methods, such as neem oil and insecticidal soaps.

3. Composting and Mulching:

Adopt composting practices to recycle organic materials from the orchard and enhance soil fertility. Mulching helps suppress weeds, conserve soil moisture, and regulate soil temperature.

Permaculture Principles in Nut Orchards

1. Diversity in Plantings:

Integrate diverse plant species within the orchard to create a resilient and balanced ecosystem. Companion planting, mixed-cropping, and incorporating nitrogen-fixing plants contribute to overall orchard health.

2. Water Conservation:

Implement water-harvesting techniques, such as swales and contour planting, to optimize water use. Design the orchard layout to capture and retain rainwater, reducing the need for supplemental irrigation.

3. Integrated Systems:

Design nut orchards as integrated systems where each element serves multiple functions. For example, agroforestry practices may involve planting nut trees alongside companion crops and integrating livestock for holistic land management.

Soil Conservation Strategies

1. Cover Cropping:

Utilize cover crops to protect and improve soil structure. Cover crops prevent erosion, suppress weeds, and contribute organic matter to the soil. Select cover crops based on their compatibility with nut trees and local climate conditions.

2. Contour Planting:

Adopt contour planting techniques to reduce soil erosion on sloped terrain. Plant nut trees along the contour lines of the land, creating natural barriers to water runoff and promoting water absorption.

3. Agroforestry Systems:

Incorporate agroforestry principles by combining nut trees with complementary plant species. Agroforestry enhances biodiversity, reduces soil erosion, and creates microclimates beneficial to nut tree growth.

Regenerative Practices for Nut Orchards

Polyculture and Guild Planting

1. Polyculture Design:

Move beyond monoculture by incorporating polyculture designs in the orchard. Planting multiple nut tree varieties, companion plants, and diverse vegetation creates a balanced ecosystem with increased resistance to pests and diseases.

2. Guild Planting:

Establish guilds around nut trees, consisting of plants that provide mutually beneficial relationships. Nitrogen-fixing plants, dynamic accumulators, and insectary plants contribute to soil fertility and pest management.

Biomimicry and Natural Processes

1. Mimicking Natural Ecosystems:

Design nut orchards to mimic natural ecosystems, fostering biodiversity and resilience. Observing and emulating the patterns and interactions found in nearby natural landscapes can guide sustainable orchard management practices.

2. Regenerative Pruning:

Adopt regenerative pruning techniques that emulate natural processes. Prune nut trees to enhance air circulation, reduce disease pressure, and promote healthy growth, aligning with the natural growth patterns of the trees.

Community Engagement and Education

1. Community-Supported Agriculture (CSA):

Establish community-supported agriculture initiatives to involve local communities in sustainable nut orchard practices. CSA programs can provide direct support to growers and foster a sense of shared responsibility for the orchard's well-being.

2. Educational Outreach:

Engage in educational outreach to share sustainable orchard practices with neighboring communities. Workshops, seminars, and farm tours can provide valuable insights into regenerative nut cultivation and encourage broader adoption of sustainable principles.

Continuous Improvement and Adaptive Management

1. Monitoring and Evaluation:

Regularly monitor the ecological dynamics of the orchard, assessing the health of nut trees, soil conditions, and biodiversity. Evaluate the effectiveness of sustainable practices and make informed adjustments as needed.

2. Research and Innovation:

Stay abreast of sustainable agriculture research and innovative practices. Embrace a mindset of continuous learning, exploring new methods that align with ecological principles and contribute to the long-term sustainability of the nut orchard.

Community and Environmental Impact

Community Engagement in Nut Cultivation

1. Community-Supported Agriculture (CSA):

Foster community engagement through CSA programs that connect growers directly with local consumers. CSA initiatives create a sense of community ownership and support, with individuals sharing in the risks and rewards of nut cultivation.

2. Orchard Events and Workshops:

Organize events and workshops within the orchard to engage the local community. These gatherings provide opportunities for hands-on experiences, educational sessions, and a deeper connection between growers and consumers.

3. U-Pick and Farm Tours:

Invite the community to participate in U-Pick events, where individuals can harvest their own nuts. Conduct farm tours to showcase sustainable orchard practices, share insights into nut cultivation, and create a transparent connection between growers and consumers.

Biodiversity Enhancement in Orchards

1. Polyculture Plantings:

Encourage biodiversity by integrating a variety of plant species within the orchard. Polyculture plantings not only support the health of nut trees but also provide habitats for diverse wildlife, insects, and beneficial organisms.

2. Wildlife Corridors:

Designate areas within the orchard as wildlife corridors, allowing for the free movement of animals. Incorporate native vegetation and natural elements to attract and support a diverse range of wildlife, contributing to overall ecosystem health.

3. Habitat Creation:

Create intentional habitats within the orchard for pollinators, birds, and beneficial insects. Install birdhouses, bee boxes, and insectary plants to attract and provide shelter for these organisms, enhancing ecological balance.

Educational Outreach on Sustainable Nut Growing

Workshops and Seminars

1. Sustainable Practices Workshops:

Conduct workshops focused on sustainable nut growing practices. Cover topics such as organic orchard management, permaculture principles, and regenerative agriculture techniques. These workshops empower participants with practical knowledge for sustainable nut cultivation.

2. Seminars on Biodiversity:

Host seminars that emphasize the importance of biodiversity in orchards. Explore the role of diverse plantings, habitat creation, and wildlife corridors in fostering resilient ecosystems. Illustrate how biodiversity contributes to pest control and overall orchard health.

School and Community Programs

1. School Outreach Programs:

Collaborate with local schools to introduce students to sustainable agriculture. Develop educational programs that include orchard visits, hands-on activities, and curriculum-aligned lessons on the environmental and agricultural aspects of nut cultivation.

2. Community Gardening Initiatives:

Initiate community gardening projects that involve residents in sustainable nut growing. Provide guidance on establishing community orchards, sharing resources, and implementing environmentally friendly practices.

Online Resources and Webinars

1. Webinars on Sustainable Nut Cultivation:

Host webinars that reach a broader audience interested in sustainable nut cultivation. Cover a range of topics, from soil health to biodiversity enhancement, and engage participants through interactive Q&A sessions.

2. Educational Resources:

Develop online resources, including articles, guides, and video tutorials, to serve as educational tools for those interested in sustainable nut growing. Make these resources accessible to the community and beyond to promote widespread knowledge sharing.

Community and Environmental Impact Assessment

1. Impact Evaluation:

Regularly assess the impact of community engagement and sustainable practices on both the local community and the environment. Evaluate changes in community awareness, participation, and environmental health.

2. Feedback and Collaboration:

Solicit feedback from the community and stakeholders to assess the effectiveness of educational outreach and community engagement efforts. Collaborate with local organizations, environmental agencies, and educational institutions to enhance impact assessment.

Growing nuts sustainably extends beyond orchard management to the positive influence a nut-growing community can have on the environment. By engaging the community in nut cultivation, enhancing biodiversity within orchards, and conducting educational outreach programs, growers contribute to a more sustainable and interconnected local ecosystem.

Beyond the Orchard: Recipes and Nut-Based Products

Culinary Uses of Nuts

Cooking with Different Nuts

1. Almonds:

Almonds add a delightful crunch to both sweet and savory dishes. Roast them for salads, blend into almond milk, or use them ground in desserts like almond flour-based cakes and cookies.

2. Walnuts:

Walnuts have a rich, earthy flavor and work well in salads, pasta dishes, and baked goods. Toasted walnuts can be a savory topping for yogurt or a sweet addition to oatmeal.

3. Pecans:

Pecans lend a buttery, slightly sweet taste to various recipes. Use them in pies, salads, or as a topping for cereals. Candied pecans are a delightful snack or dessert component.

4. Hazelnuts:

Hazelnuts bring a unique, nutty flavor to both sweet and savory dishes. Ground hazelnuts are excellent in pastries, while chopped hazelnuts enhance the texture of salads and vegetable dishes.

5. Cashews:

Cashews offer a creamy texture when blended, making them ideal for sauces, dips, and dairy-free creamy desserts. They also work well in stir-fries and as a topping for soups.

6. Pistachios:

Pistachios add vibrant color and a distinctive flavor to various dishes. Crushed pistachios can be used as a crust for meats, while whole pistachios elevate the texture of salads and desserts.

Creating Nut Butters and Oils

Nut Butters

1. Almond Butter:

Make almond butter by blending roasted almonds until smooth. Enjoy it on toast, as a dip for fruits, or incorporate it into smoothies and desserts.

2. Peanut Butter Alternatives:

Explore beyond traditional peanut butter by creating alternatives with other nuts. Cashew butter, hazelnut butter, and walnut butter offer unique flavors and nutritional profiles.

Nut Oils

1. Walnut Oil:

Cold-pressed walnut oil adds a rich, nutty flavor to salads, dressings, and even desserts. Drizzle it over roasted vegetables or use it as a finishing touch for soups.

2. Almond Oil:

Light and subtly sweet, almond oil is versatile. Use it in baking, sautéing vegetables, or as a base for homemade salad dressings.

Incorporating Nuts into Everyday Recipes

Breakfast

1. Nutty Granola:

Create a homemade granola using a mix of your favorite nuts, oats, and dried fruits. Enjoy it with yogurt, milk, or as a topping for smoothie bowls.

2. Nut-Infused Pancakes:

Add chopped nuts to pancake batter for a delightful crunch. Serve with maple syrup and fresh fruit for a wholesome breakfast.

Lunch

1. Nutty Salad:

Toss together a vibrant salad with mixed greens, sliced fruits, and a variety of nuts. Top with a citrus vinaigrette for a refreshing lunch.

2. Nut Pesto Pasta:

Blend nuts, herbs, garlic, and olive oil to create a flavorful nut pesto. Toss with your favorite pasta for a quick and satisfying meal.

Dinner

1. Nut-Crusted Chicken or Fish:

Coat chicken or fish with crushed nuts before baking or pan-searing. The nut crust adds a tasty and crunchy layer.

2. Stir-Fried Nuts and Vegetables:

Add a handful of nuts to stir-fried vegetables for an extra burst of flavor and texture. Serve over rice or noodles for a complete meal.

Desserts

1. Nutty Brownies:

Incorporate chopped nuts into brownie batter for a deliciously textured treat. Walnuts, pecans, or hazelnuts work particularly well.

2. Nutty Ice Cream Sundae:

Sprinkle crushed nuts over your favorite ice cream flavor, add whipped cream, and drizzle with chocolate or caramel sauce for an indulgent sundae.

Nut-Based Beverages

1. Nut Milks:

Make your own nut milk by blending soaked nuts with water and straining the mixture. Almond milk, cashew milk, and hazelnut milk are popular choices.

2. Nut Smoothies:

Enhance your smoothies with a boost of nutrition by adding a spoonful of nut butter or a handful of nuts. Combine with fruits, vegetables, and your choice of liquid for a satisfying drink.

Nut-Based Snacks

1. Trail Mix:

Create a personalized trail mix by combining various nuts with dried fruits, seeds, and a touch of chocolate. It's a convenient and energizing snack.

2. Nut and Fruit Energy Bars:

Make homemade energy bars with a mixture of nuts, dried fruits, oats, and a binder like honey or nut butter. Ideal for a quick and nutritious on-the-go snack.

Nut-Based Products and DIY Crafts

Making Homemade Nut Milk

1. Almond Milk:

Start by soaking almonds overnight, then blend them with water and strain to create smooth almond milk. Add a touch of sweetness or flavor with vanilla or dates.

2. Cashew Cream:

Create a rich and creamy cashew cream by blending soaked cashews with water. Use it as a dairy alternative in coffee, soups, or desserts.

Crafting Nut-Infused Beauty Products

1. Nutty Scrubs:

Combine finely ground nuts with sugar or salt and a nourishing oil (such as almond or coconut) to create exfoliating body scrubs. The natural oils in nuts help moisturize the skin.

2. Nut Oil Perfumes:

Infuse nut oils like almond or hazelnut with your favorite scents. Use the infused oil as a natural perfume, applying it to pulse points for a subtle, botanical fragrance.

Utilizing Nuts in DIY Projects

1. Nut Shell Crafts:

Get creative with nut shells, using them in crafts such as mosaic art or creating decorative items like coasters. Painted walnut shells can make charming miniature containers.

2. Nut Shell Candles:

Repurpose larger nut shells, like halves of walnuts or coconut shells, into candle holders. Fill them with melted wax, add a wick, and create unique, natural candles.

Nut-Based Home Products

Homemade Nut Butter Soap

1. Nut Butter Soap Bars:

Combine finely ground nut butters, like almond or shea butter, with glycerin soap base to create nourishing homemade soap bars. Add essential oils for fragrance and additional skin benefits.

Nut-Based Cleaning Products

1. Nut Oil Wood Polish:

Craft a natural wood polish using nut oils like walnut or almond oil. Apply to wooden furniture for a lustrous shine and protection.

2. Nut Shell Abrasives:

Utilize finely ground nut shells, such as walnut or almond, as natural abrasives for cleaning surfaces. They work well for scrubbing pots, pans, and surfaces without causing damage.

Nut-Based DIY Gifts

1. Nutty Gift Baskets:

Create personalized gift baskets featuring an assortment of nuts, homemade nut products, and nut-infused crafts. Add a touch of elegance with a beautifully crafted nut oil perfume or a jar of homemade nut butter.

2. DIY Nut Beauty Kits:

Assemble DIY beauty kits with ingredients for crafting nut-based beauty products. Include recipes, essential oils, and packaged nuts for a thoughtful and creative gift.

Nut-Infused Culinary Gifts

1. Flavored Nut Oils:

Gift homemade flavored nut oils, infused with herbs and spices, for culinary enthusiasts. Rosemary-infused walnut oil or chili-infused almond oil adds a gourmet touch to dishes.

2. Nutty Baking Mix Jars:

Layer jars with pre-measured ingredients for nutty baking mixes. Include a recipe card for nut-infused cookies, muffins, or pancakes for a delightful homemade gift.

Nut-Based Decor

1. Nut Shell Planters:

Transform hollowed-out nut shells into miniature planters. Grow small succulents or herbs in these charming, eco-friendly containers.

2. Nut Shell Centerpieces:

Craft unique centerpieces using a variety of nuts. Combine them with candles, flowers, or other decorative elements for eye-catching and natural table decor.

Sustainable Nut-Based Lifestyle

1. Nut Shell Composting:

Utilize crushed nut shells as a composting additive. The shells provide organic material, aid in aeration, and contribute to overall soil health.

2. Nut Shell Mulch:

Grind nut shells into a coarse mulch to use around garden beds. The mulch helps retain moisture, suppress weeds, and gradually breaks down, enriching the soil.

Nut-Inspired DIY Art

1. Nut Shell Mosaics:

Create intricate mosaic art using variously colored and shaped nut shells. Arrange them to form patterns or images for a unique and textured piece of art.

2. Nutty Sculptures:

Fashion sculptures or three-dimensional art pieces using nuts as the primary material. Combine different types and sizes of nuts for a visually interesting and tactile creation.

CONCLUSION

In the initial chapters, we delved into the principles of nut cultivation, understanding the varieties of nuts, and planning and nurturing your orchard. We embraced innovative growing techniques, learned to overcome challenges, and nurtured a thriving community that shares knowledge and passion for nut cultivation.

Beyond the orchard, we ventured into the kitchen, discovering the culinary versatility of nuts. From breakfast to dinner, desserts, and beverages, we explored the endless possibilities that nuts bring to our plates. The creation of nut-based products and DIY crafts extended our appreciation for nuts, not just as a source of nutrition but as a medium for creativity and sustainability.

The sustainable practices discussed in this book emphasized the interconnectedness of nut cultivation with the environment and the community. From organic orchard management to engaging the local community, enhancing biodiversity, and promoting educational outreach, we recognized that the impact of nut cultivation extends far beyond the boundaries of the orchard.

The concluding chapters took us on a journey of crafting nut-infused beauty products, incorporating nuts into DIY projects, and exploring nut-based home products. We marveled at the versatility of nuts as they found their way into cleaning products, beauty regimes, and even thoughtful DIY gifts. The sustainable lifestyle choices presented, such as composting nut shells and utilizing them for mulch, reinforced the idea that nut cultivation can contribute to a regenerative and eco-conscious way of living.

As you embark on your own journey into nut cultivation, may this book serve as a guide and an inspiration. Whether you're a seasoned grower or a novice enthusiast, the world of nuts offers endless opportunities for learning, creativity, and community building. Nurturing your orchard is not just about cultivating nuts; it's about cultivating a connection with nature, fostering sustainable practices, and sharing the joy of homegrown bounty with those around you.

As the seasons unfold and your orchard blossoms, may the fruits of your labor be a testament to the care, dedication, and love you've poured into nurturing nature's bounty. Here's to the flourishing orchards, the delectable dishes, the sustainable crafts, and the vibrant communities that grow from the roots of nut cultivation.

Happy growing, harvesting, and savoring the abundance of nature's gifts. May your orchard thrive, and may the journey continue with the promise of new growth and endless possibilities.